LIFE CRISPIES

...Come Taste and See Reality Poetry

LIFE CRISPIES

...Come Taste and See Reality Poetry

SHARON FALLOON

Requests for permission to make copies of any part of the work should be submitted online at
sharonbrownfalloon.com

Library of Congress Cataloging-in-Publication Data

Falloon, Sharon © 2012

Life Crispies...Come Taste and See Reality Poetry / Sharon Falloon

ISBN 978-0-9891275-3-0

Cover Design / Sharon Falloon

First Edition

NEW YORK

ACKNOWLEDGMENTS

This author is grateful to Almighty God for revealing the true purpose of my life; that I've experienced such passion for something beyond anything else, is priceless and my spirit is satisfied.

Thank you!

My husband Tony, my beautiful daughter Sasha and my son Jesse, for being you! Your encouragement, suggestions, insightfulness, ideas, and, most of all, your love and support, have kept me balanced.

My sisters: Marcia Constable, Angela Shaw, Michelle Leon and Yvonne Falloon. How did I get such a blessing? Family doesn't come any better than you!

My sister-friend Margaret Andrade, for your amazing loyalty! Knowing that I can call on you at any time, day or night (and I do), is heartwarming! Thank you for thirty-seven years of true friendship!

Father Mastine Nisbett. You told me that in times of adversity: you grow the most; you discover true friends; and, it's when you must exercise the most faith because God will never abandon you. You were right on all counts! Thank you for your spiritual guidance and unceasing prayer.

EDITING AND PUBLISHING

To the team for the excellent editing, publishing and business services you provided on this project.

Editor: Sasha Garcia, M.A.
Editor: Paula Panter

Cover Design: Sharon Falloon
Graphics: GOTGRAPHX

Author's Thought!

I agree. There probably is nothing left to write about that has not yet been written. No thoughts to be expressed that have not yet been expressed. Still—I write because they are my thoughts; my self-exploration; my interpretation of life.

I find it intriguing that I look at the same picture as many others and see a different perspective. There is no right or wrong—I think.

I've met a few people who find poetry confounding, complicated and, some said, even boring. There are genres in every field of art and I believe that there is a place for what I call *story/reality-poetry.*

I write simple poetry with interesting characters and characterizations; some poems are satirical; others are the result of true stories and personal experiences; and, some are inspirational, whimsical and hopefully funny. Most of all it's written to be entertaining, clever and interesting, to bring you back to the joy of poetry.

I am gratefully inspired by her majesty, Maya Angelou.

So, here I begin my spin on things.

Sharon Falloon
March, 2013

For Ruby...

My mother; my heart! You inspire me every day!

CONTENTS

PART 1

Crunchibles:

PART 2

Reality Bites:

PART 3

Introspection:

PART 4

Life hurts but I rise:

PART 5

Only human:

Crunchibles

BLANK PAGE

This blank page wears that come hither look
Enticing me to embark on a journey
Come my mind, explode my mind
To fill it up not with waddle!

It's perpetual—ongoing
Turn the page—it is blank!
Come my mind, explode my mind
To write so much more than just drivel
So that one fateful day
I'll be able to say
I've written my best verse of poetry!

DRUG FICTION

High on crack or coke or weed
How do I criticize those on speed
When I in my little sheltered world
Have never tried any of it?

My friend she said she'd tried the weed
She got so high she thought she could fly
How do I criticize her adventurous side
When I didn't have the courage to try?

The other guy he said he'd tried
A little bit of the crack and smiled
And then he'd tried a little bit more
To try to regain the magic high;
Who am I then to criticize
The raging addiction he epitomized
When I with my little cowardly self
Did not have the courage to try?

On second thought
With some contemplation
It seems to me that I may be mistaken
For certainly it took a lot more gumption
To resist the appeal of the whole drug commotion
And stand up tall for my *own* strong conviction
To *just say no* to all the temptation!

*****

James 1:12
Blessed is the man who endureth temptation: for when he is tried, he shall receive the crown of life, which the Lord hath promised to them that love Him.

Remember when:
The Cosbys were the model family; and
Little Joe and Adam made Bonanza history?

Remember when:
That Peyton Place
Pushed the envelope of risqué; and
Dynasty's high drama
MegaMoguls of their day?

That's the past—an old performance
Long ago, that was the scene
When Alexis was Delilah
Not for real—that Queen of mean!

Comes now the newest genre
Of what we love to see
Risqué's new definition
Of the brazen and the mean:

Like Teresa and that NeNe queen,
Kim W and Vicky G
The MegaStarring-Housewives
Brainchild of Andy C;

Shah Reza's old grandmother and
The incomparable Miss GG
Strong and angry women
For real—the Queens of mean!

5

Finding love is hard to do
Enter that Patti Stanger
If you tell her how you roll
She'll be your own matchmaker!

Losing weight—well, who could guess
You'd do it for television?
Yet, only for a bit of dough
You lost your inhibitions!

But the Kardashians dominate the screen
With beauty and high fashion
The new risqué they put on blast
Everyone's an icon!

Even if wack, nothing held back
They'll leak the whole damn mission
Ready, set, all systems go
For reality television!

Pazyryk culture
Polynesian mana
Japanese magic—full body suit
Samoan tatau—looks like silk

>Soldiers
>Sailors
>Circus jugglers and clowns

Otzi the ice man—57 in a row!

Criminals display it!
Father Moses embraced it!
Egyptians ritualized it!
Ancient Romans, well...they banned it!

Ye shall make no cuttings on your flesh, Leviticus
often pleaded.
Rude, dirty and covered with pictures Ibn Fadlan
– he despised it.

It's on necks, tongues, and even faces
Palms, knees and Tahitian black asses!

>Rebellionation
>Characterization
>Spiritualization
>Religionization

Fascination
Medication
Magication
Brandation
Decoration
Illustration

It's

INKART

VASHTI'S REBELLION?

(From the Bible -KJV – The Book of Esther)

"I am Vashti, the Queen of your kingdom
I demand your respect as your wife and a woman
I will not come before you Ahasuerus
Until you show me, show me some honor.

I'm tired of your chauvinistic demeanor
Of being nothing but your trophy adornment
I am a person with feelings, a woman of worth
I'm not here just to, just to do your bidding.

I do not care if it seems I'm rebelling
I'm a woman of stature, of presence, of value
Why don't you come to me with your personal
wishes
Instead of treating me, treating me like a servant?

I don't care that you're angry or petulant
That's your prerogative to be shocked, at my
disobedience
You care more for lords and them arrogant
princes
And their thoughts, *their* thoughts of my supposed
rebellion!"

Or she could have felt ill – had a case of the blues;
Had an ocular migraine or even the flu;
Or maybe she decided she'd tired of "queening"
Standing in the shadow of a debaucherous king!

Or maybe she thought she'd send a clear message
To women in the kingdom of many provinces
To fight for their rights and their own upliftment
Grow tall in their journey and resist domination.

Who knows what she thought
No clear explanation
Of why she was resistant
To go be with her husband!

Or maybe it had little to do with Queen Vashti
It may simply have been the way of The Master
To introduce a new queen, the one with a mission
To introduce a new queen, named Hadassah
called Esther.

he's sure of himself *and* his future
he designed it to be perfect, like him!
he made himself, he's convinced of it, he is:

god_man

judge of all people and jury too
scientific genius
dr. who
atheist
agnostic, and
wizard true, he is:

god_man

he walks the city 'cause he owns it you see
chin up, eyes averted: no look lesser beings
he owns the oilfields and the mines of black coal
breeds arabians and thoroughbreds
on ranches of gold.

he gets around in private jets
that's customized for his royalty
he's supreme, like a king
epitomizing deity, he is:

god_man

. . . . .

11

It started in his brain
The headache - amazing
Blurred vision and nausea
Blood vessels exploding:

                    Instant
                    DEATH!
                He is no more;
                Only hu_man
                 To the core!

Close your eyes
Turn around
Turn my world
Upside down!

Turn around sexy Adam
And give me a glance
Then train me on vocals
And give me a chance.

Turn around brother CeeLo
And give me a chance,
To display all my talents,
I'll even dance!

No right no wrong genres
All music counts
Contends Ms. Christina
Authority on voice!

Too unemotional
Sing from your heart!
Pick up the tempo
And no pitchy parts!

Show me your beauty
In body and voice
If you meet that criteria
You'll be Blake's first choice!

Open eyes take a look
Take a look and choose me
'Cause for sure I'll rejoice
If you make me TheVoice!

Came the Ska, Jamaican Ska;
But we had to get ready,
For that rhythmic rocksteady,
As we slowed down the beat
To make it more…heady;
Beginning the rise to that awesome, strong reggae
Part of the definition of our bountiful history!

Depicting a land that was violence-free,
The musical icons were proud to agree
Like:
Ernie and Glen
Stranger Cole and…some others
They sang of the freedom from Kingston to
Hanover.

Rita and Marcia and Judy—I-3s
The talented trio of Sly and Robbie;
Peter and Bob and Bunny—those three,
Transitioned their music to the incomparable
reggae beat!

But the times they were a-changing for rude boys
from shanty towns,
No work brought out their anger, spreading fear to
those around!
And di lootin' and di shootin'
Became the anthem of Trench Town!

But good soon followed evil
The best was yet to come as many the musical
icons made Trench Town their humble home,
Manifesting heart-wrenching music
That soon would be world renowned!

Jamaica,
West Indian island
Small in size, but not in stature
Continues to grow its fine music,
With horizons seeming unending;
The smooth reggae sound
Will always abound
Because the great legends revere it!

TRÈS MISÉRABLES

He takes himself so seriously
…the miserable man
Knows, sees and believes everything
He creates in his own mind;

Wife in a tizzy
Because he's so dizzy
With his grand affectation
And selective imagination;

Crumbs on the countertop
Cups in the sink
No milk in the bottle
Oh my…it just stinks!

He sees it as lazy
And it all drives him crazy.

He once was so sexy
Not a care in the world
Then came the house warden
And changed the whole swirl!

WINTER ROW

(Children's Park-2012)

Roots upside down
Reach for the sky
Spider wood
Symmetrical points
Against blue skies
I am more beautiful
No that's me!

Ballerina arms
Fifty strong
Reach for the sky;
Ballerina fingers
A thousand strong
  Gracefully bend
  Sway like this
  Dance like that
  Then, be still!

Skeleton wood
Bears sometimes;
Intertwined fingers
Overlapping the wood
Naked, but only for a time!

MY SHADOW

(for Chace)

Look at my shadow, the little boy said
Mesmerized by its elusiveness
He turned
It moved with him
Am I real?
Or is my shadow?

He perched on the bench
Red plumes arresting
Nature's black-lashed,
Black-rimmed,
Bespectacled eyes,
Peered all around him curiously!
Cocked his head to the left
Cocked his head to the right
Listening to sounds only he was discerning.
Who's in there, I thought
He seemed so interested;
Who's in there, I wondered
Could it be, my father?

So many had supped on its elegant platter
Feeding grandmothers with layers of pasta, and
rich creamy sauces made with churned yellow
butter.

It didn't care who ate on its beauty
Remembering nothing of its clay or mold making
Or even its glazing or decorating embossing.

Simply existing unknown to itself
Simply existing to please someone else!

Companion silver pieces equally uncaring
Three to the left and the right of its setting
Multi-mouths apparently expected
To dine on its fine, decaled, white porcelain!

Excited, delighted, she glowed in his arms
The handsome black stud with the sexy brown
eyes
They'd met at the auction
He'd bought the old Ford
Ended up on the backseat
Ha! Maybe in love!
The adrenalin rushed to her head when he said,
With that baritone lilt to his sensuous voice,
*"Say my name, pretty mamma, c'mon, say my
name"*
'Cause even though she was racking her brain
She couldn't remember that his name was…
Dwayne.

POPULAR GUY

I've always wanted to be popular
My handsome face renowned
Be on everyone's speed dial
The star on the late, late show!

My opinion would be sought
For every possible cause
I'd party until five a.m.
Every chance I got
Having all the girls in a tizzy
About my significant lot!

I've always wanted to be popular
The answer to everyone's prayer
Have a million dollars in the proverbial bank
'Cause I'd worked very hard for the money.

I've always wanted to be popular
Fully embracing life's flavors
With no eventual regrets, not a one
About not being popular!

Leathery rough yellow exterior
Pitted in its effervescent texture
Oil glands with limonin found in its rind
Segments perfectly aligned
To the lines in its spine!

Cut open it shines
Even seeming to glimmer
Its carpels resemble
The Maple-leaf flower
Protecting sweet vesicles
With parchment-like layers!

The twists of its exocarp
Decorative in effect
The juice of its locules
Citric in taste
Aromatic expulsion of bergamot flavor--
With a grind
Characteristics of the berry with the
Leather-like rind!

UNACHIEVABLE!

Oh triumphant pedestal
You stand so tall and true
They look up to you and dare to hope
To stand on your unrivaled perfection!

Regards, oh ye sacred halo glow
Your rings of light do shine so bright
They look up to you and dare to hope
To wear your radiant perfection!

Salutations to you, oh medal of gold
You gleam in rapturous victory
They look up to you and dare to hope
To achieve your unmatched perfection!

INTERRUPTED...102912

Hummin' along
A well-oiled machine
Diamond stud livin'
Inheritance comin'…

Life in abundance
O thrillin' existence!

TV blarin'
Radio boomin'
Piccaninnies screechin'
Mothas a cookin'…

Life in abundance
O thrillin' existence!

Party on 'til mornin' come
Drink up the Cristal
East fish-roe caviar
'Nother 'morrow, not far…

Life in abundance
O thrillin' existence!

No Sandy storm
Though causin' harm
Can change that rhyme
With a little…time!

Life in abundance
O thrillin' existence!

POWER...IT'S ELECTRIC!

(Hurricane Sandy—Part II)

Water fed
      filled with power
Wire led
      telling the hour
Of our existence

…it's electric!

Turn it off
      see its power
Everything stops
      no telling the hour
Of our existence

…it's electric!

Insidious effect
      affecting man power
Left against right
      all split asunder

…it's electric!

No electricity:

      No cable TV!
      No Starbucks coffee
            nor hot cup of tea!
      No jamboree!

No festivity!

Oh! How we cower
  when there is no…power!

…it's electric!

Continuous longing for joyous fulfillment…

Gnawing desire…
Keep reaching higher…

No satisfaction…

Sweet contemplation…
Relentless anticipation…
Can't reach satiation…

This passion…oh my!

Reality Bites

FALSE ALARM

Death comes but once in a lifetime,
Of dreams about tomorrow
(That's promised to no one).

.....

He treads definitively towards its certainty, afraid
of its finality its eternity;
Yet enjoying the bitter sweet taste of today's
living
Knowing in the back of his mind that it's
inevitable; and he wonders how it will all come
about.
But he does not squander life's precious moments,
He abandons morbid thinking, until the future.

A throb in his temple—could it be a brain tumor?
A pain in his side—could that be kidney failure?
Is the future here already?
He feels waves of tingles from the crown of his
head to tippy-toe numbness.
End of his season?

He's distracted by the 'mums and the baby's
breath flowers
Sitting idly in the expensive hand-blown glass
container
Beautiful initially, 'til the brown overcame it:
brown water, brown stems, brown petals of its

end, the stench of its demise overpowering the
parlor.

What's next in the conundrum of not being? The
unanswerable recurring question in this theme!
Curiosity overcomes the fear of the unknown
Subtexts in the saga of continuity!
Dust to dust but dust is not dead
As seeds thrive from the energy of its zest,
Bearing fruit in fine flowers: the ethereal rose, the
pungent pelargonium,
Reminds of life! Is!

Not yet, the epicedium!

Ugly:

>Nuclear blast
>>In search of domination
>Kill the children
>>Spread canceration!

Ugly:

>The sword of Genos cide
>in search of *perfection*
>swastika of hate
>Heil Hitler-Lucifer
>Germany – six million…died

Ugly:

>Genos cide!
>Bosnia – two hundred thousand…died
>Darfur – two hundred thousand…died
>Nanking – three hundred thousand…died
>Rwanda – eight hundred thousand…died
>Turkey – one and a half million…died
>Cambodia – two million…died
>Soviet Union – seven million…died

Ugly:

>Judging …race
>Judging…color
>Judging…size
>Judging…another

Ugly: lustfulness
Ugly: addiction
Ugly: pedophilia
Ugly: incest

Ugly:

          No education
          Religious discrimination
          Political indoctrination
          Relentless starvation

Ugly:

          It's so Ugly!

ON MY WAY TO HEAVEN

I dream about not dreaming about
That literature test I flunked years ago
I stand at the edge of the recurring precipice
With my heart in my throat
Can't remember the lyrics!

I perpetually dream
About being rich
Not overwhelmingly so
Just enough to buy the Ritz
With a little left over
For a place in St. Kitts!

I dream about
Having a self-cleaning house
With no vacuum cleaner, no brooms and no mops
A robotic gardener
To do the grounds rounds
Its pristine appearance
Would be renowned!

I dream about a trip to Romania
Cruising the Mediterranean
And making some stops
In an extended expedition
On the way to Australia
With additional stops
In Denmark and Armenia!

FISH HUNT

Mother's womb…it's just the beginning
Nine months gestation to come to fruition
Catapulted painfully into a world—no
compassion!

His name is Royalty
Blue blood diamond heart
Attended academies
Born to a great start!

His name is Insignificant
Born to the projects
Attended schools of hard knocks
In a world, not his choosing!

Yet, the Ivy League lawyer
Abhorred his great start
Had no satisfaction with
What he felt in his heart
There had to be, he was thinking
More to life than just…living!

Who would ever have thought
Legal Aide was the choice
That this blue blooded Royal
Would make from his heart?
But that's what he wanted
For the rest of his life
To help the less fortunate

He'd found his new voice.

Insignificant had travelled down the tubes of his
life;
Stealing, drug dealing, even pimping his wife!
That's how he landed himself in a bind
With nowhere to turn, he was losing his mind.

But there was a rainbow in the midst of his cloud
He'd landed Mr. Royal his legal-aide spouse
The beginning of a friendship
As the north met the south!

Another legal rumble
Royal knew of his stumble
But he wouldn't judge
He'd just give him a hand
To show some improvement
And adopt a new plan.   .
It would not be easy but he gladly agreed
To *all* Mr. Royal's demanding decrees!

· · · · ·

Big fish eat little fish…
The scourge of mankind
When the haves find their conscience
They could help the have-nots!

Like
Oprah
& Fitty
Angelina
and Brad
Bishop TD and Serita Jakes
William and Melinda Gates
Roger Federer-the tennis ace
Taffi & Dr.
Creflo D
Joel Osteen
& Joyce
Will-I-Am
he did his
part &
don't
forget
about
George

HAPPINESS QUOTIENT

The child laughed hysterically
With no reason why
Beautiful innocence
As if he were high!

He danced on the floor
His joy pure and loud
As he screamed from the pleasure
Of rolling about!

Joy comes so easy
When you're only four
Joy comes so easy
Sheltered to the core!

THE INDOMITABLE TEACHER BROWN

(for Ruby-2012)

A perfect red apple for the conscientious Ms.
Brown
But don't be fooled by that beguiling sweet smile
A disciplinarian she is of the young, and the
grown:
"Sit up straight…stop wriggling"
"Stop sniveling it's not about winning, it's about
the game and how you're playing"
"Today you wipe the blackboard clean"
"Stand in the corner and lift one knee,
 Hold that position 'til you learn to be meek"
"One at a time you'll each have a turn
 Sit back be quiet and learn to be patient"
"You can do it"
"Keep on trying"
"Never give up"
"Take it up a notch"
"You can be who you want to be
You can do what you want to do."

"Pull up your pants for it's not attractive
 Rebellion can be so often destructive
 Channel your pain into something constructive."

"Embrace that you're different
Don't let that define you
Character's what's important
Remember, you're beautiful."

41

"It's music day—Express your soul,
Some think the world is made for fun and frolic, And so do I! And so do I!
Close your eyes and listen
As it mellows your mind
It's the voices in unison that work as a team
Tenor soprano alto and bass
Each is important to the harmonious theme."

She smiles disarmingly at the PTA meeting
The issue of budgets is just not appealing
To those who already are experiencing a beating
In *their* own circumstances of hard living
But yes she must…discuss it you see
… for the children come first
…and they're listening.

Everyone looks to her for direction
In control of their children's future;
An authority on growth
They know it takes a village
And so   …they trust her.

The indomitable teacher brown!

FIRST PRESIDENT

(They said the Titanic was unsinkable)

They said it could not happen
Not in our lifetime, that's what they said
That a black man could become president
Of these our United States!

Our forefather Martin Luther
Disagreed with what they said
Predicting instead it'd be sooner
Much sooner than anyone said.

Martin Luther, himself a contender
Brilliant mind—charismatic persona
But, the role wasn't his
It would not be *his* future
As the task very clearly
Was geared to another!

When Jesse appeared
Now, it seemed to be possible
His rainbow coalition resonated with many
As he railed about
Man's inhumanity to his brother!

But the time was not then
As he could not deliver
God had other plans
For the coming of some other!
Born to twin cultures,
The irony, apparent

Yet carefully chosen to represent every people;

His name caused a stir
Again, how ironic
That God chose an African to be his own father
As he contended with ridicule
Because of that drama!

Still he embraced it, ignoring the jeers
Using no nomme de guerre (which would have been pointless)
As he faced the long battle
Full steam ahead!

Still, but of course,
Controversy was inevitable
As his politics became known—
Immediately invincible!
Attractive, brave, a genius he is
A man of the people, his mission robust
Putting God first, without contemplation
Of who might object to his Plan to be just!

It was all very clear
The stars in alignment
As he faced the great challenges
Not seen in eons!
He willingly accepted the mantle we gave him
As we sang and we danced
And stirred up a great fervor
For the first, very first
President Barack Obama!

They said it couldn't happen
Not in our lifetime, so they said
That a black man could become president
Of these our United States!

ANGELS AMONGST US: THE FIREMAN'S MIRACLE

(9/11- a true story; the names have been changed)

My friend came to visit me simply to say hello. It was just another ordinary Tuesday. Instead it became 9/11, and there was nothing ordinary about that now infamous day.

The shouting was unsettling—what the heck was going on? *A plane just flew into the Twin Towers,* was what the voices were saying.

Turn on the radio, we must find out what's going on, I said to my friend. Two planes had flown into the towers and they were now on fire. People were trapped in the heights and bowels of the imploding buildings and everyone was trying to help get them out before they totally collapsed.

The firefighters of the closest unit were dispatched to the towers. They went in. *Oh my God,* my friend said, *that's where my nephew, Patrick, is; he's a fireman.* Her fears were apparent—there was no reason to believe he would not have been with them. There was no way to know if he was with them—not then, not right away.

Hold my hands, I said to my friend, *and let us say an intercessory prayer for Patrick:*

46

Our father who art in heaven hallowed be Thy name, Thy kingdom come Thy will be done on earth as it is in heaven. Give us this day our daily bread and forgive us our trespasses as we forgive those who trespass against us. And lead us not into temptation but deliver us from evil. For Thine is the kingdom and the power and the glory, forever and ever. Amen.

God we put Patrick's life into Your hands at this very moment in time.

Hours later we heard that he had missed his truck and although he had valiantly tried to catch up with his unit, he could not.

And they all perished when the towers came down.

Our prayers had been heard and answered because at the exact time we were praying for Patrick, he had missed his truck.

Angels amongst us, they're here all the time, the messengers of God, they are guarding our lives.

*****

St. John 4:52-53
Then he enquired of them the hour when he began to amend. And they said unto him, Yesterday at the seventh hour the fever left him. So the father knew that it was at

the same hour, in which Jesus said unto him, Thy son liveth.

ANGELS AMONGST US: REFLECTIONS ON IRENE

Hurricane Irene roared into New York City on Sunday, August 28, 2011, with much ado. When it was first forecast that the storm was coming, I didn't believe it would really happen. But then it did hit and started moving up the east coast, with a very sure vengeance. Long Island, especially the south shore, was right in its path of destruction. The meteorologists finally got my attention that this was really happening, and so I ran out to stock up on everything from flashlights to Jamaican spice bun and some cheddar cheese.

The stores were a zoo. There was a cross in my mind between hysteria and curiosity as to how much damage this storm would wreak upon our fragile island.

Suddenly, I realized that it had arrived. The trees were doing more than just rocking in the wind, and the rain was coming down in pelts. It was like nothing I'd ever seen. This had not happened in New York for a long time, you see. Blackout! The electricity went as I watched the trees blowing in the breeze! The candles gave the room a warm yellow glow and my angel-brother's pillar-candle, winked twice, as it signaled he was there watching over whatever transpired.

For me, it became a time of reflection when I looked up into the deep-red orange sunset and began to write poetry – the one poem spurring on the invention of the other.

The children were agog with pleasure at: the lack of electricity, thus, the personal flashlights forming rings on the ceiling; the glowing candles with smoke on their tips; and, being wrapped up tight in their grandmother's aura. It was a time for the history books – Irene seen through the eyes of innocence. They had no fear – there was no reason to be afraid – though they did not know it, they were safe and secure.

*****

Angels amongst us, they're here all the time, the messengers of God, they are guarding our lives.

THE TEMPEST

(August 28, 2011)

The storm arrived in all of its grandeur
It screamed up the shore
Wreaking havoc as it lingered
In its eventual departure!

Hysterical and shocked
The cherry rose trees
Trembled and danced in the unexpected breeze
The electrical pole stood out like a thumb
'Gainst the colorful backdrop
Of foliage thrashing about!

Mother-nature, how profound!

But after the storm came the miraculous calm
The blue and white sky with a hint of red color
Looked eerily like the ocean
Turned upside down!

White clouds interspersed, with touches of blue
And was that a rainbow that came peeking
through?
Like standing on land on the far side of the ocean
Watching hurrying waters
Looking up at the sky!

Mother-nature, how profound!

THAT'S ALARMING

No alarms, none were sounding
Besides silent sirens
Revealed on ears that were unhearing
Of the doom
Not far yonder…Oh 'twas alarming!

EXCRUCIFICATION

(Brother mine)

Here I stand in my kitchen, crying endless tears.
I remember the night he was dying, like it was
only yesterday.
He called me long distance, since I was way far
away.
The feeling he was feeling, was so hard to bear.
There was only silence, but I knew he was there.
He couldn't speak, no; not a word he could say.
When it gripped his equilibrium, he knew I was
there.
Breathing a breath with him, our hearts beat as
one.
No morphine could help him, no matter how
strong.
When it gripped his equilibrium, he cried along.
He was confounded by the rigor, and the torture
of its grip.
Breathe with it, breathe with it.
In through the nose and out through the bit.
Slowly, more slowly, now pant, pant, pant!
Like a woman in labor, sit up and grunt.
It didn't occur to me to give that advice.
Advice came not easy on that dreadful night.
My experience, close to death-pain!
Maybe that's so.
But somehow, most definitely, for sure I have
doubts.
Bones dissolving; body disintegrating; pain so
excruciating:

He did his final exhale.
It must be like Jesus on that Calvary tree.
When he could bear it no longer, he gave in – and died!

Grass ledges fenced in
Hiding, Protecting
Precious cargo
And
Bright metal swings

Black on Black
Blue and White
Hiding, Protecting
Concrete jungles of
Hi-rise cement
And
Red squares of
Brick-on-Brick

Black on Black
Blue and White
Hiding, Protecting
Gold Oil
Metal bullets
Diamond blood
And
Vaults of green poison

Black Helicopters
Flying high
Bright lights glaring
Way up in the sky
Hiding, Protecting

Cemented white landscapes
Black Key-holed portals
And
Mystic brown pizza
Mission ongoing

Green coveralls
Hiding, Protecting
Wide water sinkholes
Black slimy liquids
And
Ever Blue oceans

Green coveralls
Blue and White
Hiding, Protecting
Travelled routes made of tar
Hi speed iron rails
And
Their magnificent houses

Helicopters flying high
Green Coveralls
Black on Black
Blue and White
Hiding
Protecting:

Platinum lives!

THE SIMPLE THINGS

Walking the park watching your children
Chasing after butterflies of black and of yellow
In wonderment of God's creation
In charge of his treasure!

Flying red kites
With their long strings aflutter
While black collie dogs
Tag along for your pleasure.

Running along stretches of beaches
Savoring the feel of sand in your toes
Gazing blue heavens for Venus and Mars
Hoping to see a few wishing stars!

Waking up to cool morning breezes
Knowing you can linger
Just a little while longer
Snuggling between white cotton sheets!

Eyes closed as you soak
In warm bubbled water
And dream of rich and prosperous tomorrows.

Hanging out with your friends who have proven
their value
While you regale them with gratitude because of
their splendor
Sinking your teeth into crispy green apples

Drinking red wine and eating white truffles.

Meditating in solitude as you handle life's
troubles
Stretching your mind for manifesting solutions
It was that simple after all, now apparent
You dance and you sing and rejoice—it is over!

The simple things…

CHRISTMAS DAY FIRE

(Inspired by a true story that occurred in December, 2011))

Red flames lovingly licked first its needles of fir
Then its brittle brown branches, causing a stir
Silently creeping up the tall evergreen
Obliterating baubles that hung from its limbs
Slithering along hard wooden floors
Its crackling sounds almost unheard
As it climbed like an acrobat up the walls of the
foyer
Reaching up to devour its crown-molded high
ceilings
Suddenly exploding, engulfing all spaces.

The smoked-orange-plume mesmerized in its
stature
Drifting upwards and downwards in orchestrated
unison
Reverently kissing the door of the dwelling
Rapidly descending down marbled front steps
Sidling up to the manicured yellow rose garden
Introducing itself to the skilled human fighters
Too late, oh too late, for the three little maidens
…as they slept!

Use all of the senses, the body, the mind;
Bruce's philosophy for survival and life;
With his two-fingered push up, he spoke with his eyes;
The fight's of the mind, opined Mr. Lee;
Find yourself, no pretenses, and just be!

…..

The ivy-league lawyer believed in his teachings
Left the tort to his peers and embraced m.m.a.
He shares rippling muscles with an exuberant crowd.
Ready for anything, the discipline is loud.
Enter the dragon, the fight is profound
ly simple in all of Lee's preachings.

Readied for the deaths in his soon-to-be clan:
Mother, brother and Julia's child;
Life changed with the madness of a dead soul.
Adapt to your environment like water he's told,
On a dark flow with Jennifer, the academy pro
who'd met disappointment on that idol show!
God led him to save her from that madman's ire
when she stayed in his bungalow, evading disaster!

…..

Light in darkness
A new season
Two fingers can do anything
Given a reason—Rise!

Use all of the senses, the body and mind,
Lee's proven philosophy for survival and life!

MOTHER-TO-BE

Her brown eyes sparkled, like topaz gems,
remembering her inner treasure
The human being she had conceived, now
residing in her belly!
She marveled at the mystery, of the child she
would deliver
Mother, oh mother she would become, to the
journey of another!

And she wondered what it would be:

Mild natured like a gentle doe wondering
quietly through the meadow;
A body racked with emotions like a furious
tsunami;
A philosopher, a healer, a scientist, another;
Could that child grow up to be the ultimate
achiever!

She wondered.

A daunting task, this motherhood role
She couldn't take it lightly
With no experience, no schooling, no class and
no course, her challenge she knew was
enormous.

And she wondered
Could she do it?

A shining star
A vision of light to the soul emerging within
her
The pliable mind, seeking its path
Could she fulfill expectations?

Too late contemplation
The die was long cast
She scoured the annals of her tortured mind for
the answer to her dilemma
And found the consoling, relieving conclusion
that had escaped her prior rumination:

With God at the wheel
Parent supreme
She knew for sure
She could do it!

It's an unfortunate fact
There's no going back
Decisions today
Claim tomorrows;
It's not rocket science
It's as simple as that
Decisions today
Claim tomorrows!

Betcha, that handsome guy Bill,
Would give anything to have a chance to change
his decision
To throw caution to wind
And have a fling
That almost destroyed his good working.

And that slick, tricky Dick
When he listened in to plentiful, long
conversations
Betcha, on second thought
He'd take it back
And erase all his foolish decisions.

Now, Don Q, the VP
No Spelling Bee he
When he showed that he could not spell
P-O-T-A-T-O
Betcha, he'd love to go back
Give it just one more shot

To prove his intellectual mettle!

Then there was George's grand plan
Not to respond
When they told him about the tall towers
He stayed with the kids
Reading ABCs
Betcha, he'd like to change that decision.

But none can compare
When it comes to sheer gall
The decision to steal from companions
Betcha, Bernie'd change it all
If given a chance
To wipe the slate clean and start over!

It's an unfortunate fact
There's no going back
Decisions today
Claim tomorrows;

It's not rocket science
It's as simple as that
Decisions today
Claim tomorrows!

*****

Philippians 3:13-14
But this one thing I do, forgetting those things which are
behind, and reaching forth unto those things which are
before, I press toward the mark for the prize of the high
calling of God in Christ.

GUN CONTROL

(Dedicated to the victims of the Sandy Hook school massacre-12/14/12)

"Mommy, are my eggs ready yet?" Little Jenny inquired as she put on her leggings and warm, lamb's wool, apple-green, pullover sweater.

"Yes, my darling, your eggs are ready and some sweet, hot chocolate with the marshmallows on top."

.....

"I hate school, I tell you; can I please stay home, Mommy?" Sam pleaded.

"C'mon, son, don't give Mom trouble, you know you have to go."

"No, I don't want to; I want to stay home today!"

Mommy ignored his tantrum, off to school...for his very last day!

.....

"I'll go warm up the Mercedes—it's a little cold today. Give me five minutes, Zoe and John; then I'll be ready to go."

"Oh and honey, remember we see Ms. Peacock at three, to discuss Zoe's reading delay."

"Okay—and I promise, scout's honor, that I will not be late."

.....

"School bus is here, Molly-Sue, let's get going, don't keep Mr. Bob waiting, you know he can be such a grouch."

.....

66

"Thank God for carpooling; Danny said he'll take Cassandra to school today."

·····

Life as usual, nothing different today, that's what it seemed like until ten o'clock came; then all hell broke loose in the Sandy Hook school as the gun man was shooting and having his way. Now, Jenny and Sam, Zoe and John, Molly-Sue and Cassandra - they knew life no more.

·····

Some eggs and hot chocolate still sat on the sink; the words of Sam's tantrum still hung in the air; Zoe's three o'clock session was needed no more; and, carpooling and buses had cancelled their tours.

·····

How pointless the murders of twenty small children!

What satisfaction gained by ending their futures?

Evil had reared its ugly antenna but Angels surrounded their journey to heaven!

So long, to our children, now with their savior;
so long to our children, and we say *au revoir.*

I AM BELIEVING...

that the grass is green
because i've seen it
on this same side
even when it was brown
at the end of the season

that the sun will arise with the dawn's
commencing
and with bold orange hues it will set in the
evening

that the face i see in that mercurial mirror
is indeed the physical me

that there are seasons and reasons for all of the
seasons:
of love of joy of gladness and sadness
of trials temptation redemption forgiveness

that the earth is round and the oceans are deep
beyond any depth that i've ever seen

that the titanic sank when they said that it couldn't
it hit a huge iceberg and the impossible happened

that katrina destroyed a place called new orleans
a port in louisiana where i've never been

that volcanoes erupted in tamboca and pelee

killing thousands of people the worst ever seen

that dinosaurs lived in the mesozoic era
and pyramids exist in the mid-east or africa

that the ice age happened two billion years ago
and glaciologically speaking has still lingered
here
in both the northern and southern hemispheres

that moses saved the jews with the exodus from
egypt
and lincoln freed the slaves in his fight to save the
union

that Jesus Christ lives, He's over two thousand
years old
crucified by pontius pilate He hung on a tree
that He arose from a tomb, and it was on day three
and He's coming again for those who believe

that space travel's real and the challenger
exploded
and airplanes can travel from rome to california

that the twin towers fell on a september morn
when two planes destroyed them over three
thousand died

that there are 12 months in a year and 60 minutes
in an hour
and it's 4:50 in india when it's 9:20 in australia

that telephones function with no strings attached
across all the continents by simply a touch

that rain falls upon us through condensation
and droughts are spontaneous when there's no
precipitation

that i'm here for a reason
i'm part of the chosen
with blood-bought salvation
i'm the temple of God

that there are five year-old africans who weigh
thirteen pounds
and politics can be evil but love conquers all

that george washington was the victor
when we the people heard his voice
the first president elected by unanimous choice

that the fourteenth amendment equally protects all
and we pay income taxes or have trouble with the
law

that spring follows winter then summer then fall
and every knee shall bow before Him, for He's
Lord of all

that a fire and brimstone asteroid,
destroyed sodom and gomorrah
but God saved a cave in a place called zoar
so lot could escape the disaster

that history really happened though i didn't see it
it's well documented and so i believe it

that there'll be an end to this era
and, the end of the world
i am believing...que sera...sera?

Introspection

A woman leaves the land of her birth to live in a new country. She examines her immigrant status introspectively.
 (Circa 1979-2012)

JAMAICA, SWEET JAMAICA

Oh struggling land determined to be free
Blue seas, Blue Mountains
Ebbs and flows of your soul
Concealing lamentations, of your agonizing poor
Jamaica, sweet Jamaica, land of our birth.

Out of many one people, striving to be free
Challenges reflected in the eyes of your youth
That hopeful smile eluding sad eyes
Jamaica, sweet Jamaica, land of our birth.

The depths of its culture revealed in its faces
With hues of black, white, brown and red colors
Of African, European, and East Indian ancestors
Jamaica, sweet Jamaica, land of our birth.

Oh struggling land determined to be free
Your vast resources offering the way to
achievement
Come, come mighty universe purchase and
redeem
Return to God's paradise, this land of our dreams.

PERSPECTIVE

(For Ms. Jane-circa 1989)

So, you want to live in America!
So you want to live in New York!
Do you have the great foundation?
Do you know who you are?

Are you ready for the anger?
Are you ready for the hate?
This is what you face here
The trauma could be great!

You can smell the money in the atmosphere
You smell it in the breeze
You smell it in the factories
You smell it on Wall Street.

You see the money in Jerry's smile.
You see the money in Betty's walk.
You see the money in Bob's tension.
You see the money in Don's…stroke.

The fast life could really get you
Are you ready for New York?

Out of many one people
That's where you come from,
Out of many one color,
That's where you are.

Are you ready for the anger?

Are you ready for New York?

It could make you hate yourself.
It could make you hate your color.
Do you have the great foundation?
Do you know who you are?

This could be a great nation,
Most people think it is
It depends on what you're looking for
It depends on who you are.

The children must be told
The truth of their foundation
For they are citizens, born here
Whether they're ready or not!

Out of many one people
But you have to fight for your own
For they've been left out of the picture
For too long they've been shot down.

So the divisions don't work here
West Indian, African, Asian or what
All the people of color
All the people in one slot!

So each one must teach one, to
Give ourselves the great foundation, to
Give ourselves the education
'Cause you want to live in America!
'Cause you want to live in New York!

She still was reeling from the decision to
leave her native land;
the only place she'd ever known as home, a place
that she'd watched change with time, a place once
so beautiful, still beautiful, but different.
Now she was in a strange land,
with strange people and new customs.
How will she assimilate into this new and strange
land?
Yet, she agonized, aren't people just people after
all? Still, she knew it would be a challenge!

…..

She strives for <u>inner peace</u>
It's no different for her than anyone else seeking
it;
She wonders what will bring it about for her.
She knows!
When she completely accepts herself for who and
what she is
All the flaws, all the faults,
Still accepting herself
Knowing she is God's creation and part of His
grand plan;
Knowing and believing—truly believing
That she is alright
No matter what happens, it will be alright,
because
God is on her side!

She speaks of God
Believes so much in God
But does she know enough about God?
Knowledge of God is innate—His essence was in her from the moment of birth;
Always in her heart, always in her thoughts no matter what she was doing or where she was
Living; he was always guiding her!
Yet—she knows she's only beginning her journey.
It takes the ordinary person a long time, many experiences and hard trials
—And so it will be for her—
To achieve that great state of inner peace!

…..

She remembers when she was growing up
Her greatest fear—<u>mother dying</u>!
And she told her!
And her Mamma said to her, *Pray to God not to take me away until you can handle it.*
Now she was grown and still she questioned her ability to deal with her mother's death.
Her answer, not even in contemplation!
They were always physically separated—much to her chagrin—now more than ever, with her in a strange land.
But their bond was so strong, neither time nor space could alter their love for one another.
She had still been nurtured even in her longing for that physical closeness.

Then she had her own child and she wonders what *her* fears might be.

She knew of her own fears for her child. Will she allow herself to follow the path of the straight and narrow; or

Will she choose the way of the world?

Will she stay the course to become what she wants to be—her wonderful dream?

Please God, she said: *let it be, her reality.*

Then she wonders, could *her* greatest fear also be…of *her* mother dying? Hmmm!

…..

She constantly questions this state of togetherness called <u>marriage</u>

She ponders…Is this all it is about?

She doesn't know if they even have anything in common.

She fears that they'll live their lives to ripe old ages but never get that closeness which her heart so much desires.

And Affection:

She fears that someone else could give her what she needs, but

She'll never find that out

Because   … she is too scared to get out there and look around and…

She's in a new land, a strange land and so

She agonizes!

Maybe, if she doesn't keep wanting and needing

Then it could be alright!

It may just be the way of her destiny.

Yet she wishes for that feeling of comfort, so
desperately;
Of knowing that he'll be there for her—Always;
No matter what;
Not judging—just
Being there, loving her unconditionally.

…..

She fears staying too long in this…<u>strange land</u>.
She feels like an interloper although she knows
that this is everybody's land;
A fantastic, awesome but scary land,
That makes her feel totally controlled and
sometimes even helpless.
She thinks she would be very afraid to grow old
here,
Such disdain for the old!
Then she realizes that she, herself, does that on
occasion;
But always she catches herself
One day—if I'm lucky I too may be old.
And I don't want to be just respected; I'll want to
be truly accepted.

She's young and beautiful—for now!

Will she survive in this strange land?

Yes she must, for this is her home—her new
home, and she wants to be happy!

…..

UPDATE:

And she did—survive, and not just survive—but thrive! In this great land, where opportunity continuously knocks, she seized life by the balls, and worked like an ox, claiming happiness and her portion of God's own creation; and, the land *too* claimed her as its own, because of ...*her* value.

And she lived!

Life Hurts, But I Rise

MOTHER AND CHILD/WOMAN AND WOMAN

She burst from the womb
A pearl from its shell
So beautiful, so pure
Innocent to the core
Mother's breath
Caught in her chest
Almost forgot to exhale.

Time went along
The child grew up strong
Willful, yet playful and kind
Mother lost her grip
Made a few little slips
And soon lost the child to the world
(so unkind, so demanding, so wild)
Goodbye my love, goodbye.

A woman she was
With a will of steel
Yet, Mother and child forever a team
Woman and woman
So different it seemed
Yes – different through time
But not changing the theme!

For better, for worse
Woman and woman
Mother now knew
What love was about!

For nothing compared
Not even close
To having a child
Grow up in this world.

ANGELS AMONGST US: THE MIRACLE TRIP

(9/04-a true story)

I hadn't returned to Jamaica for many, many years although my family still lived there, with no intention of leaving the troubled, yet ever beautiful land of our birth; especially my brother, the legendary "Bagga" Brown. He was not going anywhere! I'd left my island home many years before because my new extended family had moved to New York.

Now, I contemplated a return to see my mother who was growing old. "You must go," my husband encouraged me, "you don't know how much time she has left."

He was right. I bought my ticket, with a lump in my throat and pain in my gut, but still I did it.

It was a wonderful reunion with my family. My fearless brother, my amazing niece, and my challenging nephew, were all there to greet me. And, my mother; when I saw her I wondered how I could have so long stayed away.

It was sheer bliss, balm to my spirit, soul and body as I hugged my family and savored the time and space of the homecoming. It had been so long, yet it felt that time had stood still, so little had changed.

I slept with my mother and thanked God for the wonderful feeling of family that I'd not remembered for a very long time.

It was on the second day of my visit that the unthinkable happened.

My brother and nephew had gone away to tend to some critical business. I enjoyed a day of restfulness with the remainder of my family while they were away and the time flew by very quickly.

Be careful of your thoughts for the thing you fear the most will come to pass.

I'd dozed off on the deep-red, love-seat sofa while the television diligently watched me.

"Don't move," said the voice from deep inside my consciousness. *A dream, perhaps*—the little voice in my befuddled mind murmured. But it was not. I awoke to the nightmare reality of an armed home invasion.

"Don't move, I said. Yuh no understand?" The men holding the guns were incensed that my brother had moved, defying their command.

"Okay, okay," my brother replied, as he stopped dead in his tracks.

"Take off all of your jewelry and hand it over to me," one of the men demanded.

"Give me the cell phones," the other man decided.

"Don' look at their faces," I implored my family, "don' look at their faces 'cause they don' have on no mask."

I could not believe what was happening. Then very suddenly, I bolted from the place where I was seated and ran to another room, but, unfortunately, there was nowhere to hide, too late I realized.

"What yuh trying to do?" the voice had followed me, "g'wan back outside *now* and lie down with the others."

My family lay on the floor awaiting our fate. The guns were drawn; next step… execution.

Really? I said to God in my thoughts. *Really? This is it? This is what you brought me here for, to realize my greatest fear?*

The click of the guns could clearly be heard— then nothing!

Complete nothingness followed. *Are we dead?*

"They gone," said the amazing woman who cared for my mother. "They left and I still have my phone, so I'm calling the police."

"Are you sure they're gone?" I asked the woman for I could not believe that my greatest fear had been realized…but not fully—I was still alive! We all were—still alive.

"Dem gone and the police coming," she announced triumphantly, as I opened my eyes to verify the seemingly unbelievable truth.

Oh God, oh sweet Jesus, you were here all the time, being with us, watching over us, lifting us up, saving us. Please forgive my doubt and my fears.

My mother emerged from her room, having slept through it all, yet she looked puzzled. "Did something happen?" she asked. "What happened?" she persisted.

"Oh, nothing much, Mamma dear, I'm just so happy to be here," I declared, wiping away my hysterical tears.

I looked around—and then I remembered.

My father, the late Baptist minister, had used this room for many spiritual ceremonies: weddings, christenings, counseling sessions, family devotions and prayer services. It had all taken place in this room where I found myself at the mercy of these two misguided human beings.

I looked all around me—the Bible was there and pictures of Jesus, the twelve disciples and my late father too. The aura of goodness permeated the air as I breathed in and breathed out the reverence of God being there.

It would be much later that we heard about the shooting incident between the police and our attackers. The chase had led them to Waterhouse in Kingston, where with guns blazing they had fought a great fight, and it really was unfortunate that they were able get away. It was eerie when I realized that the guns did work after all! Yet not one hair of our heads had been touched in the terrible drama.

Be careful of your thoughts for the thing you fear the most will come to pass.

Yet, despite that foreboding, and my very obvious lack of faith throughout the happenings, I knew in my heart that true to His promises, I had not seen God coming but I knew that He'd been there. He'd brought my family and me through the midst of the storm to complete safety.

I learned a great lesson from what had transpired. Be anxious for nothing; but in everything by prayer and supplication with thanksgiving let your requests be made known unto God and He *will* take care of you.

*****

Angels amongst us, they're here all the time, the messengers of God, they are guarding our lives.

> *Job 3:25*
> *For the thing which I greatly feared is come upon me, and that which I was afraid of is come unto me.*

> *Exodus 34:21-23*
> *Behold, there is a place by me, and thou shalt stand upon a rock: and it shall come to pass, while my glory passeth by, that I will put thee in a clift of the rock, and will cover thee with my hand while I pass by: and I will take away mine hand, and thou shalt see my back parts: but my face shall not be seen.*

THE WORD OF THE LORD

Honor Thy Mother—A Soldier's Story was written for my brother – Basil 'Bagga' Brown.

Nobody compares to him. Growing up, I didn't have an identity. I was always Bagga's little sister and it was just fine with me.

Some of my favorite times with Baz (that's what we called him), were born at Orangefield Primary School. My mother was the principal there and in order to get to school every day, there was a big hill that we had to climb. No car could climb that hill—we definitely had to walk. And so for many years, my Mamma, Baz and I climbed that hill—every day, after Daddy dropped us at the corner. Some momentous things happened to us on our travels on that hill. Like when a bulldog tried to kill my Alsatian puppy, Rex, on our walk down the big hill, through the Orangefield village, to meet my father at the corner. Baz saved my puppy and I can't remember how, since that attack dog was huge and incredibly scary! But he did—save my puppy!

Then we went to school in Kingston and had to *board out.* All of our high school years were spent in other places than home. That was tough. But my brother was never far away—he always had my back. Sometimes, all we had *was* each other—and that was enough.

He was so kind. He'd give you his last penny. It was hard for me to understand how someone could be so giving. Friends and strangers would come banging on his door for help when they were in trouble because they knew he would always help them out.

And, oh how he loved his mother! That was the inspiration for my first novel and the title of the book. It was pure, his dedication to her. Nothing stood in the way of taking care of our Mamma Ruby.

He could have been anything—lawyer, doctor, professor—you name it! But that was not his calling. He was a television icon, a radio personality, a man of the people—that's what he enjoyed and that's how he lived. His television program *Weh Yuh Seh?* captured the hearts and minds of most Jamaicans and I know you miss its ingenuity.

He was excited about my first novel and he was my consultant on the Bob Marley reference in the story.

Baz became sick with cancer in 2002 and I was heartbroken. He battled the disease for about nine years but finally on January 29, 2011, he lost the fight and went home to be with his maker.

Brother mine – I'm missing you!

MISSING YOU

Please do not be disappointed
Your spirit still lives on
Your big personality
Your brilliant smile
We have not forgotten.

Please do not be disappointed
We know how much you hurt
The decision was hard
From the very start
But we know that you had to make it.

Please do not be disappointed
Don't think that we don't cry
The hurt of your loss
Grinds the hearts and the souls
Of those who so dearly loved you.

We are not disappointed
For we know you would have stayed
And you did for a while in spite of your pain
Ignoring your true agonizing;

But then came the time
That you had to go
And so we said...*Auf wiedersehen!*

Auf wiedersehen...Auf wiedersehen!

BEST DAY

(for my father)

Clothed in white, appearing angelic
I stepped in holy water
While the spirited Baptist minister
Showed me the gateway to heaven!

C'EST LA VIE!

Can't hold onto it the day or the night
They go to return again right on time.

He died unexpectedly, the man of her dreams
Yet time marched on, ignoring her sorrow
Deliberately arriving at its planned tomorrow!

Time was!   Time is!   Time will be!

Anticipating the results of his past foolish action
She listened anxiously to someone's prognosis
Hanging off the cliff of uninvited suspicion
Awaiting with fear the real diagnosis!

If only she could go back
To when she was young
Took so much for granted…
And change!

Can't touch time
Can't go back
Can't fix yesterday
Just move on from the ashes
Of that sick diagnosis!

Time was!   Time is!   Time will be!

JUST GIVE ME ONE MORE DAY

Pickin' white cotton and plowin' cane fields
There are no dreams of an imminent free me
Only the reality of my indentured,
Tortured being;

Still, I want to live for one more day
Just give me one more day.

I'll raise all your children, cook your brown stew
I'm ready to do what you want me to do
And I won't even tell you
Of my thoughts of you
('cause that would be rude)
About you being inhuman
A monstrous soul;

Since I want to live for one more day
Just give me one more day.

It's hard to be critical of you, I suppose
You had no control of your history, like me
You learned to be brutal
I learned to bow down;

'Cause I want to live for one more day
Just give me one more day.

I'll be your subservient me for a hundred more
years

Since I'm promised a man who will help set me
free
They tell me he's an Abraham
Didn't catch his last name
But until he gets here, I'll be yours, you can
plunder;

'Cause I want to live for one more day
Just give me, one, more, day.

Close the door to the world and his influence
All sound stops.
The silence is loud in its immensity
As she gathers herself from the cacophony of loud
voices
Criticizing harshly her attempts at
progressiveness;

She's resilient!

She meditates without the loudness and
distractions
Shuts out sounds that could bombard her
consciousness
So she can think and grow thoughts and ideas;
and…

Herself!

But how long can she stay hidden from the
violence of the noise,
As she grows her thoughts and ideas into the
ultimate goal
Of wealth and affluence?

Open the door to the world and his influence
Oye—the noise returns; and people like ants,
Scamper into her stratosphere

Enabling group think, disabling her individuality and
Ability to ruminate over her deepest
thoughtfulness!

Shyness—that's impractical for her; and…she
shakes it off.

Eyes alert!

As the door to the world reopens
Her strong bones prevail;
From the meditation and prior rumination
Over deep thoughtfulness
She catapults into her true destiny and she soars and reaches
The highest stratosphere!

_____|And Oprah
        _____|Rosa
_____|Maya
|Angelina

Oh, shattered ceiling!

DREAM ON

You compare me to that Helen of Troy,
The face that launched a thousand ships
(No Nemesis me);
You, my Theseus!

You compare me to
The rubra and flava marrow of your bones,
Me the red and the bright yellow flow
Of the healthy blood sustaining your life!

You compare me to your atomic number 8,
The complicated presence in most of what is
Allowing you to breathe, you said.

You compare me to an orchid,
The testicle of your essence!
You are rooted you say, because of me.

Daydreaming and I'm thinking of you,
Comparing me to Helen and Orchids,
Marrow and Oxygen
And, I glow.

PATIENCE

Sit calmly and wait and ponder your state
That's what he told her when the troubles came
For nothing will happen by tomorrow, he said,
So you must understand that and enjoy life
instead!

Patience – a loss of control
Of what you thought was yours
The perfect time to search your soul
But the need to know preempts contemplation
As anxiety grows and fear overcomes us!

Fear that life will leave us behind
We won't make it in time
…the money
…the marriage
…the game
…the fame

Patience – a loss of control
Of what you thought was yours
The perfect time to search your soul
A time of reflection, what's life all about?

You're not here alone
A blip in the universe
So small is your role
But you *can* make a difference
Just examine your goals

Life held in abeyance
While you wait for more!

Sit calmly and wait
And ponder your state
Of emotion…devotion
Of circumstance and happenstance
Of bliss, and…the list
Patience – a loss of control
That leads to your growth.

*****

Psalm 40:1
I waited patiently for the Lord; he turned to me and
heard my cry.

Romans12:12
Be joyful in hope; patient in affliction; faithful in prayer.

Isaiah 40:31
But those who wait on the Lord shall renew their
strength. They shall mount up with wings like eagles;
They shall run and not be weary; They shall walk and
not faint.

COURAGE

(for KAF-TY)

Courage!

It first meant so little when there was no need for
it
Life was a dream
'Til it all turned to spit
And then came the time when I screamed for it.

Courage to be brave
Courage to be strong
Courage to face the demons
       Of death – Oh my father!
       Of loss – Oh my brother!
       Of anguish – for death and for loss!
       Of loneliness – from it all!

And then courage comes marching along
Reminding me there's hope
Reminding me of my faith
If I only believe
After the storm comes the calm
God's many promises of a new tomorrow.

Courage – be strong!

*****

Psalm 31:24
Be of good courage, and he shall strengthen your heart,
all ye that hope in the Lord.

DIVINE ORDER

How do you stay calm in the midst of the storm,
When your life is turned upside down,
And the punch to your gut has you doubled in
knots?
How do you continue as if nothing is wrong and
all around you is the same humdrum song?
Normal—they are!

What does normal feel like again?
It was just yesterday when sleep came so easy,
Daydreaming was fun,
Your mind could be blank without a thought of
tomorrow;
And there was… no sorrow.

How do you stay calm in the midst of the storm?
You don't…for a while
Life has changed overnight
But the new normal comes
Adapt or you die
It's not bad after all
You're alive—you can cry!

Cry
It eases the pain
Cry
It washes you clean
Cry
But then

…you must smile!

Smile
When your heart is breaking
Smile
It will start the healing
Smile
Life may be different
But it is…worth the living!

After the calamity accept the change
Look for the rainbow in the midst of your cloud
It's God's divine order in The Plan for your life.

How do you stay calm in the midst of the storm?
Seek God's intervention, you'll never find harm
While you're mourning your loss
God is changing your future
Look for tomorrow
…for it only gets better!

*****

Psalm 37:23
The steps of a good man are ordered by the LORD; and
he delighteth in his way.

Her floppy red hat reminds her of
A time she hardly remembered...
'Til now!
Of a time of not yet
When she'd not known about
The people she'd meet in her sojourn called
life.

Her passionate prom date
She recalls from a distance
Full of toothy, loud and hysterical laughter,
Returns to her mind how he'd thoughtfully
expressed
His love of her beauty and her floppy red hat!

The white Christmas times
When all through the house
Favorite carols were singing of Jesus' birth
And family communed in their best of attire
Including for her...her floppy red hat!

She hadn't remembered for a long time the
details
Of graduations and weddings and christenings
and things
And what had become of her past, now so
distant
And the whereabouts of her floppy red hat!

FRIEND

Who stands beside you
When all around fall by the wayside
When hardship befalls?
…A friend!

You said you loved me
I'll never leave you
No matter the challenge
You said – feel no fear
Who stands beside me?
…A friend

You were there in my crisis
You reminded me of my faith
You can't lose it,
That's what you told me.
Who stood beside me? You said
…My friend

You were my rock you had told me
Made from good stock, I consoled thee
Who stood by me? You said
…My friend

Then calamities came upon me
I fell on hard times
I thought – *I can handle*
Based on your sweet rhymes!
Who stands beside me? You'd said

…Your friend

But your words were so empty
Nowhere to be seen
You had no compassion
You forsook me
No strength of character
You were a fraud
Thank God almighty
He showed me who you are!

Leave the doors open
To allow the experiences of time to slip in
unannounced and the unexpected to shape the
complicated fabric of life's offerings;

Sowing seeds to ripen into the future harvesting
Of a hopeful fulfillment, not understood at the
time of its planting;
Wisdom, not usually an ingredient in the recipe,
of first time round development
One that ironically may only come with
experience
Not realized at the time of its planting, that it's
lacking;

That was then
This is now;

The fruit of the sowing manifested, if lucky
In the brightness of treasures and some shiny
objects
Or the fruit of the sowing manifested in failed
measure
Hopefully to try again, with wisdom this time
To find its true treasure!

*****

Philippians 3:13-14
But this one thing I do, forgetting those things which are
behind, and reaching forth unto those things which are
before, I press toward the mark for the prize of the high
calling of God in Christ.

She climbed down
                the
                 steps
Of the old dungeon building
The ones from hell were not more alarming!
Stainless steel tools hid in
Stainless steel vessels
Like sharpened steak knives, awaiting the carving.

LA FÉE VERTE

Who is he to tell me what I can or cannot drink?
To quench my thirst or poignant hunger
For more to life than counting chickens and
nickels
And pearls and furs and diamond encrusted gold
stud earrings.

Who is he to tell me what I can or cannot drink?
To assuage my thirst for his soul of my soul, his
heart of my heart;
When instead I find
His soul of her soul, his heart of her heart
With no hiding his affection for her!

Who is he to tell me what I can or cannot drink?
When my spirited ancestors knew of its blessings
To troubled personas some of them exhibitionists
As they mastered the science of inebriation
Ignoring the cry of the passionate prohibitionists!

Who is he to tell me what I can or cannot drink?
To help me to cope with life's unsubtle ironies
As he continues with his chick-bangin' chick-
bangin' chick-bangin'
Degrading and challenging my burgeoning
womanhood.

111

Who is he to tell me what I can or cannot drink?
When counting chicks outweighs counting chickens?
I'll drink *la fée verte* instead of the hyssop,
So I'll live another day,
Thanks to its potent insistence.

TOMORROW

Tomorrow when it's bright with the sun at its
peak
She promised herself
She'd begin to live,

Tomorrow when the shadow had passed from her
brow
She promised herself
She'd smile with the world,

Tomorrow when the tragedies had all been
forgotten
She promised herself
She'd be joyful, yes happy,

Tomorrow with its promise to give a new start
Tomorrow she'd accept it
And begin life at last.

BLESSED RAIN 6.13.12

Cloud tears abound on silver lit legs
Run like a river with no restraint;
Soothing he felt the wet drops on his face
Melding with teardrops that fell on twin cheeks,
Then peace like a river washed over his being.

PRAY

I may not now fully understand
God's supreme plan for my existence
Until He unfolds it bit by bit
To its ultimate conclusion;

Trust in me
He says to me
Very, very clearly
God has no use for mortal man
Who has no faith to believe Him!

Help me Lord to understand
That you're always right here with me
Through thick and through thin
In my highs and my lows
You've orchestrated it all to perfection!

Only Human

HOARDER (A MILD CASE)

(for Sasha)

A hundred pairs of shoes
......and still counting
Fifty pairs of jeans in all colors and sizes
She can't get rid of any, it would not be wise
Every inch of her closet is covered with
something
That is valuable and needed for
......Just in time dressing!

The makeup bin's full
......And, it's overflowing
With mascara, eye-shadow, nail clips and skin
ointments.

She's not superficial
Not what you might think
She's agonized carefully
About what's important
There's not one thing she has, you see
That's not essential for her sanity
She shudders to think she might have a problem
'Cause there's no way for her to find a solution
She cannot, just cannot give up her possessions!

Does hoarding define some kind of madness?
C'mon—that's stretching the imagination!

SLEEP, KIP, DOSS

He trustfully enters sleep's merciful gate
To an unknown pathway he'll never remember
Fairly sure of his imminent return
After sojourning in unfamiliar places;

The buzzing sound of his snoring rest
Cuts through the startled air like a saw;
And his unconscious arms reach out to touch
With unawareness of their frantic, blind pawing;

He laughs out loud, speaks to invisible souls
While the rumbling sounds of his flatulence
Leaves the still startled air, agape with its stench!
And his half-open, unseeing, unblinking eyes
Eerily resemble those of the dead;

As he walks safely through a land of green
pastures
He gladly lies down beside the still waters
Fearing no evil thing
Caressing grass carpets
As he is, asleep within sleep!

Brief respite this, this kipping venture
Journey into a recurring oblivion
Easily achieved no aids to slumber
He's at peace, free to roam
through the annals of time
Until he returns to his space, just from habit

unscathed, restored, refreshingly invigorated
Only to do it again, once he tires.

‹PERFECT

(For Whitney)

What an achievement – Perfection
…Like Jesus.
But we aren't.
And those who proclaim it
Fail—in time
Because we're just human

Show me the one who made himself
Those delicate eyes
That organ of smell
Those sensuous lips
And beautiful smile

Show me the one who made himself
In the image of God
That perfect man
But you cannot claim it
For no human can

That's the beauty of life
To strive for perfection
In the image of Christ
A goal for achievement

And when we fail
God gives us the courage
To rise up again
To try to attain
That ultimate marriage
Of perfect and human!

WITHOUT SIN

Never stole a dollar from your mamma's purse
ever
Never took a glimpse at your friend's test paper
Never daydreamed about your neighbor's wife,
Nester
Never thought someone else's grass was way
greener
Never exalted yourself — "I am better"
Never lived in a glass house, you're no squatter

Always give unconditional love to your "brother"
Always give to the poor and some other
Always give glory and praise to another

Then throw the first stone—you're perfect,
remember?

*****

St. John 8:7
He that is without sin among you, let him first cast a
stone...

He approached the building with anticipation
Knowing she stood by the window
The beautiful Virginia besotted with him
Sought to fulfill him with fervor!

She saw him approach the building
She stood by the window just chilling
Repulsed by his presence thus steaming
But obligated by her commitment to another
Acted out the role of true…lover!

He was mesmerized by the swish of her hips
Her deep sultry eyes
Drew him to their depths
Her sensuous mouth and kissable lips
Held him captive to return for another…kiss!

. . . . .

She was a slave to him and his whims
Because she loved only…him
He owned her soul, possessed all of her
Romancing her to total surrender!

. . . . .

He arrived at her door with expectations
So sure he was of her devotion!

Look into her eyes
          Look into her eyes…and see!

He's renowned for his affluence
Possessing *all* of his choosing
She's lucky to have a man of his breeding
And he knows, she knows
        He is her blessing!
                        . . . . .

She'll do whatever to please him
So that she can please…him
Her only beloved
Her one true love for she is besotted*!*

She'll do whatever to please him
Even marry…another
So that she can please…him
Her only beloved
Her one true love for she is besotted*!*
                        . . . . .

Look into her eyes
        Look into her eyes…and see
That she does not belong to thee!

But you can only see
        Her physical being!

Wise eyes should see how she looks
        Beyond your hemisphere
                Whenever you're near!

Look into her eyes
        Look into her eyes…and see

That she *does not* love thee!

In the beginning God created heaven and earth
and everything in it:
Light and darkness
Valleys and streams
Birds Cows and Sows
And the colors of spring:
    Russets and oranges
    Lilacs and pinks
    Fuscia and marigold
    Sky blue, apple green
Towering redwoods reaching up to the sky
Dwarfing tall evergreens stunted by far
Perfection   …and nothing talked back.

Finally, then God made man in God's image
God did it last - thought about it a lot
And gave him free will
But wasn't long you see that God had to be mean
rearranging the scene
Driving Adam and Eve off the Eden property
'Cause they'd eaten from the forbidden tree.

God knew it would happen
Because God is God
And gave him free will
Exalting him for a chance at pure goodness!
But no way …he was disobedient!

God created man last

Agonized the decision
But God knew, just knew he'd screw up
　　　…and he did
And boy was God mad.

Endless days of hard labor in
　　　Coal mines　　cold factories　　hot offices
　　　Outdoors in cold weather
　　　Outdoors in hot weather
Women in hard labor to birth another
　　　They multiply
　　　　　— In twos and threes and even
　　　sevens sometimes through his brilliant
　　　ideas of science and technology —
　　　But in pain and in sorrow!

And thousands years later
There's still no improvement.
Somehow he found a way
To be worse than ever, still operating with pure
bad behavior:

Killing him brother, like Cain had killed Abel
Dominate one another, like the Jews and that
Pharaoh
Thief from each other, like Jacob from Esau

Just making God mad
Forgetting 'bout Noah!

Tsunamis Earthquakes　　Hurricanes　and
Tornadoes
God mad again

No doubt about that!
God's last great invention
Man made in God's image, screwed up
　　　…again!

Man that is—not God!
God can't screw up
And man from God's Spirit can't screw up either
…Because of redemption!

*****

1 John 3:9
Whosoever is born of God doth not commit sin; for
God's seed remaineth in him; and he cannot sin, because
he is born of God.

SPIRIT

I am
    not me
Spirit
    not self
    nor emotions
    nor feelings
I exist
    soul and body

But—

I am

Spirit!

FAITH

He has the power of Jesus in the palm of his hand
Power bestowed by the Master Himself
Power to move mountains
Still the winds and the waves
To walk on sea waters
If he only believes!

See that no man know it HE said to the blind men
HE had just cured, but they didn't listen and they
went and told the whole world and brought HIM a
dumb man and HE cured him too; then later some
guys said to HIM that they only had five loaves
and two fishes to feed five thousand people in a
multitude and the Jesusman just blessed the food
and fed everybody with plenty leftovers; and
another time it was four thousand people and
there were plenty leftovers then too; and then
some people brought another blind man this one
from Bethsaida since, apparently, two weren't
enough, and asked Him to touch the man, so HE
spit on his eyes and HE did it twice before the
man could see really really good, and HE told him
not to tell anybody but bet you he did; and then at
some lake called Gennesanet, Simon and his
friends couldn't catch any fish all night long but
when the Jesusman said *let down your nets for a
draught,* then the ship was full of fish and they
had to get another ship just to hold everything;
and then a poor widow from a place called Nain
lost her only son and HE said to her *Don't cry* and
HE told the dead kid *Arise* and he sat straight up
and hailed HIM up; and then HE cured the
woman who couldn't stand up straight for
eighteen years, and the man with the dropsy, both
on the sabbath day and made everybody all angry
but HE explained it away and said *The Son of man*

130

is Lord even of the sabbath day; and right after
that HE healed the man with the withered hand
making it look good just like the other one, on the
sabbath day again; and then ten lepers begged him
to cure them in some Galilee village and HE did it
but only one of them came back to say thanks and
his faith made him whole; and HE healed the
Malchusguy whose ear some people did cut off;
and the centurion's servant in a place called
Capernaum who was suffering from the palsy and
was in great pain and Jesus told the centurion *I
will come and heal him* but the guy didn't think he
was worthy enough for Jesus to come to his crib
and so HE told him it was okay since he believed,
and his servant was healed in that very instant;
and then, HE went to a wedding in Cana and
because HIS Mamma Mary asked HIM, HE
turned a whole heap of water into the best wine
ever so much so that the hostguy said they had
saved the best wine for last 'cause the first batch
never tasted that good; and in Cana too HE healed
some nobelman's son when HE said to the
nobelmanguy *thy son liveth,* and he did, and HE
wasn't even in the same room as the boy; but the
sick man by the pool at the sheep market in
Bethesda, was there for thirty-eight years trying to
get up enough strength to be the first one to dive
into the pool, so he could get better, but he was
always too slow and somebody else always beat
him to it, so he said anyway, and in exasperation
Jesus said to him *Rise, take up thy bed and walk*
and he believed HIM and he did take up his bed
and he walked; and then some cat named Lazarus

from Bethany dead for four days and stink, stink, stink, was raised from the dead when Jesus said *Lazarus, Come forth* and even though he was tied up in grave clothes, he came out of the grave like a mummy, and they had to loosen his garb and then he was fine; and there was somebody's maid one time that HE raised up from the dead too, during her own funeral, then HE told them that she had only been sleeping; and another woman had touched HIS garment and HE felt it and because she believed that she would be healed from a blood disease that she had for twelve years, HE turned around and told her *Daughter, be of good comfort thy faith has made thee whole*; then another time, HE was in a ship with HIS disciples and up out of nowhere came a great tempest and Jesus was sleeping when they came running to tell HIM about the storm and HE said to them *Why are you fearful?* and HE spoke to the wind and the sea like how they talked to each other and the men couldn't believe that even the winds and the sea obeyed HIM; but best of all was when they saw HIM walking on the water and because Peter believed when Jesus said *Come,* he too walked on the water, for a time anyway, 'til he started to doubt a little bit, and then he lost the power, and nearly drowned; and then, another time Jesus killed off a fig tree right on the spot; and he showed some people that they could do the same type of things if they believed like tell a mountain to go jump in the sea, and it would; and after that HE did many many more miracles and all of them happened because the people believed;

and then, HE promised one last miracle, that *Whoso eateth my flesh and drinketh my blood hath eternal life and I will raise him up at the last day.*

JESUS POWER (MML&J—THE MIRACLES)

(This is a Jamaican patois version)

See that no man know it, Jesus tell the two blind man dem that HIM just cure, but yuh tink sey dem listen? No, instead dem went and tell di whole world and den dem bring a dumb man fi HIM fi cure and HIM cure him too;

then later some guys sey to HIM that dem ongle had five loaves and two fishes fi feed five tousand people in a multitude, and the Jesusman just bless the food and feed everybody with plenty plenty leftovers;

and another time, it was four tousand people and dat time again there was plenty plenty leftovers;

and den some people bring another blind man since two wasn't enough, dis one come from some place called Bethsaida and ask Him fi touch di man, so HIM spit on di man eye dem, but HIM had to do it twice before the man could see really really good, and HIM tell him not to tell nobody, but yuh tink sey him listen, no way;

and den at some lake call Gennesanet, Simon and him friend dem couldn't catch any fish all night long, but when the Jesusman said, *Let down your nets for a draught,* den the ship full a fish, and dem had to get anotha ship just fi hold everyting;

134

and den a poor widow from a place call Nain, lose her one son and HIM sey to her *Don't cry* and HIM tell di dead kid, *Arise,* and him just sit right up, straight, and big up Jesus;

and den, HIM cure di woman who couldn't stan up straight fi eighteen years, and di man with the dropsy, both a dem on the sabbath day, and mek *everybody* all up in arms, but HIM explain to dem sey *The Son of man is Lord even of the sabbath day,* and right after dat, HIM heal di man with the withered hand and mek it look good good good just like di oder one, on the sabbath day again;

and den, ten leper dem beg him fi cure dem, in some Galilee village, and HIM did it, but ongle one of dem come back fi tell HIM tanks, and fi him faith made him whole;

and, den another time, Jesus healed wan guy name Malchus, whofa ear some people did cut off, for real;

and di centurion's servant in some place called Capernaum, who was suffering from di palsy, and in a ole heap a pain, and Jesus tell the centurion, *I will come and heal him,* but di guy didn't tink he was worthy enough, fi Jesus fi come to him crib; and so Jesus tell him it was okay since him believe in HIM, and him servant heal up same time Jesus sey dat;

and den one time, HIM went to a wedding in Cana and because HIM Mamma Mary ask HIM, HIM turn a ole heap a wata into di bes wine ever, so much so, that di hostguy sey, dem save di bes fi last, cause the first batch never taste good like Jesus own;

and in Cana too, HIM heal some nobelman's son, when HIM tell di guy sey *Thy son liveth* and him live, and HIM wasn't even inna di same room as di bwoy;

but di sick man, by the pool at the sheep market in Bethesda, was dere fi thirty-eight years tryin' fi get up enough strength to be di firse one fi dive inna di pool so him could get betta, but him was always too slow and somebody else always beat him to it; so him sey anyway, and in exasperation Jesus sey to him, *Rise, take up thy bed and walk,* and him believe HIM, and him did tek up him bed…and walk;

and den, some cat name Lazarus, who come from a place call Bethany, dead fi bout four days, and him stink, stink, stink, raise up from di dead when Jesus sey to him *Lazarus, come forth,* and even though him was tied up in some grave clothes, him come outta di grave like a mummy, and some people had to loose up him clothes and den him was fine;

and den, there was somebody maid one time, that HIM raise up from the dead too, during her own funeral, den HIM sey dat she was ongle sleepin;

and den, anotha woman touch him clothes and HIM felt it, and just cause she believe, HIM heal her, from some blood disease dat she did have for 'bout twelve years, and when shi touch HIM, HIM turn roun' and tell her, *Daughter be of good comfort thy faith has made thee whole;*

den another time, HIM was in a ship wid HIM disciple dem and up outta nowhere come some big ole tempest, and Jesus was sleeping when dem come running fi tell him bout di storm, and HIM sey to dem, *Why are you fearful?* and HIM talk to di wind and di sea, like how dem talk to dem one anotha, and the man dem couldn't believe, dat even di wind and di sea obey HIM;

but best of all, was when dem see HIM walking on di wata and since Peter believe him could do it, when Jesus sey, *Come,* him walk on di wata too, for a time anyway, 'til him start fi doubt a little bit, and den him nearly drown;

and den, anotha time Jesus kill off a fig tree right on the spot; and him show some people dat they could do the same tings if dey believed, like tell a mountain fi go jump inna di sea, and it would;

and after dat HIM did many many more miracles
and all of dem happened because the people dem
believed; and den, HE promised one last miracle,
that *Whoso eateth my flesh and drinketh my blood
hath eternal life and I will raise him up at the last
day.*

AGORAPHOBIA

I rather stay at home all day
In my studio apartment
Than go to 42nd street
And face its yawning spaces
For no apparent reason
Than to say
That I had done it!

The shoe's hangin' on
For Wall Street to recover
Bringing back from the dead
Those valiant martyrs who sacrificed golden lives
for the price of bad stocks,

The shoe's hangin' on
For the soldier of hate to make a move
So it can negate the traumatic effects on
unsuspecting targets,

The shoe's hangin' on
Reminiscing about the good old days
Of cotton pickin' enriching the massa
Who cared for his cattle harvested from the
bowels of ships
In total objection to the end of that era,

The shoe's hangin' on
For it's not been that long
Since the right didn't know what the left hand was
doin'
When there was no unemployment
So genos cide was applauded
Wreaking the vengeance of one race on another:
"How could you not know that we're
disappearing, while you stroke our diamonds,
caress our furs and make light of the gold that you
steal from our mouths,

now toothless,"

The shoe's hangin' on
Observing: mind-raping; unequal standing;
The spirited killing of all the unworthy;
Those held in bondage carrying papers
Hopefully to prove they're free and thus worthy,

The shoe's hangin' on
Awaiting change, to drop,

CUCKOO

cuckoo cuckoo
cuckoo cuckoo

I knew when it happened (the separation of
myselves) and
I allowed it to come naturally, embracing the edge
Crossing over, observing life from a distance
Through the eyes of another…

cuckoo cuckoo
cuckoo cuckoo

Another who understands me better than my
original myself
Giving me strength to cope with hard places;
What hard places—there are none anymore
Through the eyes of another…

cuckoo cuckoo
cuckoo cuckoo

Another who understands me better
Speaking for me in dire circumstance,
Smiling about the happy times,
Weeping when there's sorrow; and
As it gets more complicated
Look, here comes another…cuckoo!

NO PROBLEM MON!

(C'mon get a job!)

Impatient she listened, to his tears of
discontentment
About his chosen profession, daydreaming
Inconsolable, because he hadn't won the lottery
Resigned to the thought,
Of his own unemployment!

NO HATE!

Hate.
So strong an emotion, so vile
The thought that it could be in you
Repulses your soul
Yet there it is, there it is
Eating away at your core

How can you reconcile hate
With the love of God
You say that you have within your heart?
It cannot be done, cannot be done
It is an oxymoron

Look at it face to face
Evil comes in all shapes
It comes to change your heart, change your heart
But only if you let it

Call it out, what it is
So you do not become it
Pride and jealousy – stare them down
And say, *you have no dominion over me, over me*

Declare God's Plan
Mysterious and wise
It's revealed state by state, state by state
And it does not include…hate!

RUMOR HAS IT

Better days are coming, that's what they say.
But I don't believe it
I've heard that before.

They say there's a cure for every disease
If that is true, then where is the proof?
For surely, for sure
We didn't withhold
The antidote remedy that reverses the poison;
The aspirin, that relieves the erythematosus;
The Langerhans' insulin, that attacks diabetes;
The vaccination, that prevents poliomyelitis;
The antibiotics that help cure encephalitis.

Surely, for sure we wouldn't withhold
The medicinal potions
that would help so much more
And make us shout
from hospital rooftops
That we *had* prevailed
and cured *all* diseases!

It's not about the stained glass windows; nor
The well-maintained gold mausoleums for
platinum bluebloods who died various deaths
eerily resembling ordinary men; nor
The fine crystal chandeliers enlightening the
sanctuary; nor
The mahogany pews given by a benefactor; nor
The millions of dollars found in the ample Church
coffers; nor
The silvery tongue of the PhD minister; nor
The religious Sunday worshippers regaled in their
splendor.

It's not about the material grandeur; nor
The perfect souls who have found their way
home!

Surprisingly it's about
The Church without walls; and
The relentless field mission to find
Its lost souls!

*****

James 5:20
Let him know that he which converteth a sinner from the
error of his way, shall save a soul from death.

146

JOURNEY

(For Niko and Chace)

Life is a journey it's true
Completely different for me and for you
A unique experience
So hang on tight
For it could be…A real bumpy ride!

Expectations – that's natural
Reality – may be different
Hopes and dreams
Go – Pursue them
But fate is the precursor
Of what becomes real.

Don't forget to pray
Every day
For what you long for could be in God's plan
But what if it isn't, you must understand
Don't be disappointed, go on with the hand
That God has dealt you, remember the Plan.

It may take an era
To get the whole picture
But be patient, my friend
Someday you'll understand.

An adventure in time
Don't make it so serious
Write the songs that rhyme
And the books for the curious

147

Take care of the orphans
And give to the poor
And always be meek
In whatever you seek!

Pursue engineering
Or teaching too
A medical doctor
It all starts in school
It's a part of the journey
That will make you…you.

Don't rush through the process
Enjoy life's successes
But expect the hard places
That's when you'll stretch
To your full potential
Courageous and tall!

Life is a journey, it's true
Completely different for me and for you
A unique experience
So hang on tight
For it could be…A real bumpy ride

And at the end of your journey
Let's hope you can say
Life was an adventure
And I remembered to pray
With few regrets
And much pleasure
Every part came together
To make me…A Winner!

ABOUT AGING

I'll buy the Steinway grand piano
That I have always wanted
With no regard to where it sits
There must be a place, for sure it will fit
Doesn't even matter that I can't play a note
The lacquered black color will make it look dope.

Don't mind if I sit in my old rocking chair
For hours at a time if I want to
There ain't no place that I have to go
And certainly not in a hurry
I make my schedule on a whim
I've become quite the woman of leisure.

I'll drive my car any way I please
Don't need your commentary
All the folks down at the DMV
Have approved my driving habits!

Don't think you're gonna rip me off
Because I may look feeble
I'm packing heat in my little black purse
And I've become quite trigger-happy.

Stop your jeering and mocking of me
Because of my dozing habits
I'll take a snooze at the drop of a hat
To filter out mindless drivel!

I take my aging with a grain of salt
Confounded that I'm still here with you
I'm eternally grateful for all of my years, and
The wisdom that's come with experience!

SISTER, SISTER

(A True Story)

The two were together all of their lives
Through thick and through
thin that's how they survived
Sisters they were born,
best friends they became.

Time came and time went

And they grew even closer
One family they were
When the little ones joined them
True blood to the core
No extended family
Their goal—to adore!

And… time marched along

Now the children were grown
With lives of their own
Sisters back together
To live in one space
But the strain of survival
Had taken its toll
They couldn't find loving
They once just adored.

More time passed between them

Then the day finally came

I've lost all my family, one sister declared
They've all gone abroad
And I'm still in mourning
Dear sis, think about it ...
Can I come home?

Of course, of course, the other decided
But she just wasn't sure at the time she committed
For she was so stressed
With her own life tests
And then she remembered...
Sister, sister
Through thick and through thin
No room for resentment
Stick it out to the end
Forget hesitation
And be a good friend.

As time marched along
They tried to stay strong
But the strain of their livin'
Was causing bad feelin'
Could it really be
Was it plain to see
That they'd grown apart
And there was no new start?
The silence grew louder
As they pondered their thoughts!

Then came the illness as if to say
If we can't be closer I might as well go away!
The deterioration was rapid with no one to stay
Depression...inevitable

Still yet…she prayed
But nothing could help her
When pneumonia took over
It came with a vengeance to slay her
That killer!

Goodbye darling sister
Goodbye my best friend
I wish it were different
And you were here instead
Oh my how time changes the things we once
loved
But I'll meet you in heaven where I know we will
find
Only better tomorrows…and no end of time.

WHERE'S THE STING?

(Excerpt from the novel: Honor Thy Mother-A Soldier's Story)

She lay in her casket so quiet so still.
Peaceful and angelic—she's no longer here.
In her two-piece beige dress made of flawless raw
silk
Her make-up's impeccable with dust colored lips
and her closed eyes reveal mascara-eyelashes.
Her recent manicure displays perfect cuticles
with amber-rose polish, the finish is gleaming.
Not one strand of her lightly teased hair is
misplaced
on her stylishly coiffed, well-positioned blonde
head.

She's beautiful, even in death…hallelujah!

"Good-bye darling grandmother and thank you for
caring.
Your unconditional love has truly sustained me."

Her emotion gripped her as she walked away.

The professional mourner parodied a broken
faucet
As she wailed her fine tribute to the
unforgettable…Claudette!

*****

1 Corinthians 15:55
Oh death, where is thy sting, Oh grave where is thy victory.

FORGET-ME-NOT

You went away inside yourself
And I wasn't there to be with you
To savor your precious lucidity
And remember your ebullient personality.

Our time of bonding seemed so brief
It slipped away just like a thief
As we pursued dreams that precluded each other
Not finishing the puzzles we started together.

The telephone calls were not sufficient
To bridge the gap of time and space
The letters we wrote helped my heart to believe
That we beat the challenge of the eternal rat race!

Yet only time helped us realize
The loss we endured by being apart
Time we'll never retrieve nor revive
Gone like the wind with no new start.

No tears, no dreams, no hope for tomorrow
None can console me and quench my sorrow
You went away inside yourself
And I wasn't there to be with you, *Mother!*

Oh to be them, I want to be them.

Them with the palace that sits on the hill
boasting white marbled floors and faucets of gold;

Them with the historical family tree
Two boys, two girls and a puppy named Bree;

Them who's as beautiful as that Elizabeth Taylor
With the violet eyes and skin looks like powder;

Them with the influence that comes with the
power
To have others do what they want for their
pleasure;

Them with no fear, no fear of tomorrow
For their lives have been perfectly, perfectly
sculpted;

Oh to be them, I want to be them.

'Cept, the house on the hill holds cold souls like
its marble
austere, uninviting, translucent, yes, daunting
the ears of its walls often cringe at the anger
expressed on its texture by a motherless father
whose influence over others is godless, thus
cheap;

That beauty like Elizabeth's, it's only skin deep
shallowly hankering after diamond tiaras
with a continuous obsession to be Mrs. Joneses,
She's hardly one to be emulated!

Oh to be me, I want to be me
A loving heart designed for God's pleasure
Beauty from within, that comes in due measure
Oh to be me, I'm glad to be me!

The way that he treats her like the Queen of Sheba
The way that he treats her like there is another.

The jubilant feeling from having a newborn
The jubilant feeling when baby is grown.

Life in its heyday at age thirty-five
Life when it's over at anytime.

Only for a time
It's only for a time!

OLYMPIAN

You're the best of the best, magnificence on
display
Discipline abounding, all else laid aside
Life in abeyance four years in a row
Medals of gold, your ultimate goal!

Why you and not me of talent apparent?
From the day of your birth, destiny predetermined
You climbed to the ceiling by the time you were
three
Olympian in the making, still I ask, *Why not me?*

Phelps the torpedo cuts through treated waters,
Reminding of great whites coming in for the kill;
Gabby D, flying squirrel, mesmerizes in flight
Smile of an angel, sting like a bee;
Usain, lightning bolt, defies comprehension
Speed of the cheetah, fastest alive;
Oscar P, double amp, in a league of his own
Undaunted spirit, courage defined!

Go on great Olympian
Your grace overwhelms
Your skill none can fathom
Muscles of rock,
Mind of steel
Majestic creation
You're God's *masterpiece*!

*****

Genesis 1:27
So God created man in His own image, in the image of
God created He him: male and female created He them.

But that's not how I remember it
Or is it?
It could be, but
It seems a little hazy now.

No, that's not how it happened
Or was it?
Could be I remember it differently
That's what I think.

Now I remember
That's exactly how it happened
I'm pretty sure of it
Yes, I'm positive…I think.

Pervious bleached sand
Looks like finely pressed powder
Hugging undulating edges
Of see-through sea waters;

Woody brown limbs of regal, tall oak trees
Frame cumulus-clouded celestial skies
As breaking dawn seeps through jigsaw spaces!

Leather-bound books grace mahogany-wood
shelves expectantly awaiting inquisitive paired
eyes to believe in tall fables,
Their mantra—the willing suspension of disbelief,
With bespectacled wonder of stories' conclusions!

Words—boldly ambulate on black-lined
parchment pages
Chronicling tales of passion and sorrow
Creating art, embellishing anger
Soliciting characters for classic bestsellers!

BIBLICAL REFERENCES

King James Version of the Bible

*****

Drug Fiction
James 1:12

Vashti's Rebellion
Esther Chapter One

Angels Amongst Us: The Fireman's Miracle
St. John 4:52-53

Angels Amongst Us: The Miracle Trip
Job 3:25 & Exodus 34:21-23

Patience
Psalm 40:1, Romans 12:12 & Isaiah 40:31

Courage
Psalm 31:24

Divine Order
Psalm 37:23

Then/Now
Philippians 3:13

Without Sin
St. John 8:7

Createman
1 John 3:9

Cathedral Essence
James 5:20

Where's the Sting
1 Cor.15:55

Olympian
Genesis 1:27

RESOURCES

Just Say No
First Lady, Nancy Reagan, 1982

Big Fish Eat Little Fish
Pieter Bruegel the Elder, 1557, From the Heilbrunn
Timeline of Art History. Pieter van der Heyden

Funiculi, Funicula...*Some think the world is made
for fun and frolic, and so do I, and so do I.*
Peppino Tarco, Luigi Denza, 1880

It Takes a Village
Ancient African Proverb; "It Takes a Village"
Hillary Clinton, 1996

Daydreaming
Lyrics and song by Aretha Franklin, 1972

Smile
Charles Chaplin, John Turner, Geoffrey Parsons, 1954

...Sting like a bee
Muhammad Ali

A Coney Island of the Mind
Some of the work was inspired by the poetry of
Lawrence Ferlinghetti, 1958

Freedom Papers
University Library System